JUST SWING

Progressive piano solos

GW01471582

ARRANGED BY STEPHEN DURO

Chester Music
(A division of Music Sales Limited)
8/9 Frith Street
London W1V 5TZ

PREFACE

Here are 16 tunes carefully chosen from the repertory of swing 'standards'. Playing these arrangements calls for particular interpretative skills; here are a few suggestions to help your performance.

Rhythmical numbers should aim to set the foot tapping. In many cases this can be achieved by subtly accentuating the second and fourth beats in a bar. Groups of even quavers ♫♫ should generally be played as if written 𝅘𝅥𝅮𝅘𝅥𝅮 - known as 'swung'. On the other hand, songs in slow tempi should be played 'straight' (with even quavers) more often than not. Some of the ballads make use of rich harmonies and all such passages should be unhurried.

The songs are arranged according to difficulty, with the easier pieces (approximately Grade II to III standard of the Associated Board) appearing first, and the harder ones (Grade V/VI standard) towards the end. Fingering, where indicated, is intended as a guide only and should be altered to suit the needs of individual players.

Stephen Duro

Visit the Music Sales Internet Music Shop
at http://www.musicsales.co.uk

This book © Copyright 1997 Chester Music
Order No. CH61281 ISBN 0-7119-6439-4

Music processed by Allegro Reproductions.
Cover design by 4i Limited.
Printed in the United Kingdom by Caligraving Limited, Thetford, Norfolk.

CONTENTS

NICE 'N' EASY

Words by Marilyn and Alan Bergman
Music by Lew Spence

Play this arrangement in an ultra relaxed way.
The dotted crotchets (beginning at bar 5) do
not need too heavy an accent.

Moderately

17 F E Am
22 Am♯7 Am7 C Em7♭5
26 A7 Dm G7aug C
31 Caug F E Am
f
36 D7 C Cm Dm G7 C

LAZY RIVER

Words and music by Hoagy Carmichael and Sidney Arodin

This arrangement calls for a relaxed style of playing. Try to shape the melody by giving a slight accent to the top note(s) in a group, e.g. the fourth note in bar 5, and in similar places.

13
D7
G7
16
B♭6
Bdim
F
D7
1.
19
G7
C7
F
D7
G7
C7
F
N.C.
2.
23
G7
C7
F
D7
G7
C7
F
mp

THE LONESOME ROAD

Words by Gene Austin
Music by Nathaniel Shilkret

This song does not not want to be played too slowly: try to keep the music flowing in a relaxed, gentle style.

17
E♭ Cm7 Fm7 B♭7 E♭
21
Am7(♭5) D7 Gm Am7(♭5)
f
26
D7 Gm Edim Fm7 B♭7 E♭ E♭7
mf
31
A♭ A♭m6 E♭ Cm7 Fm7 B♭7
35
1. E♭ Fm7 B♭ N.C.
2. E♭

ON THE SUNNY SIDE OF THE STREET

Words by Dorothy Fields
Music by Jimmy McHugh

The jauntiness of this song can be enhanced by keeping the left hand accompaniment subservient to the melody. For example, avoid placing an accent on the second note in the left hand in bar 5.

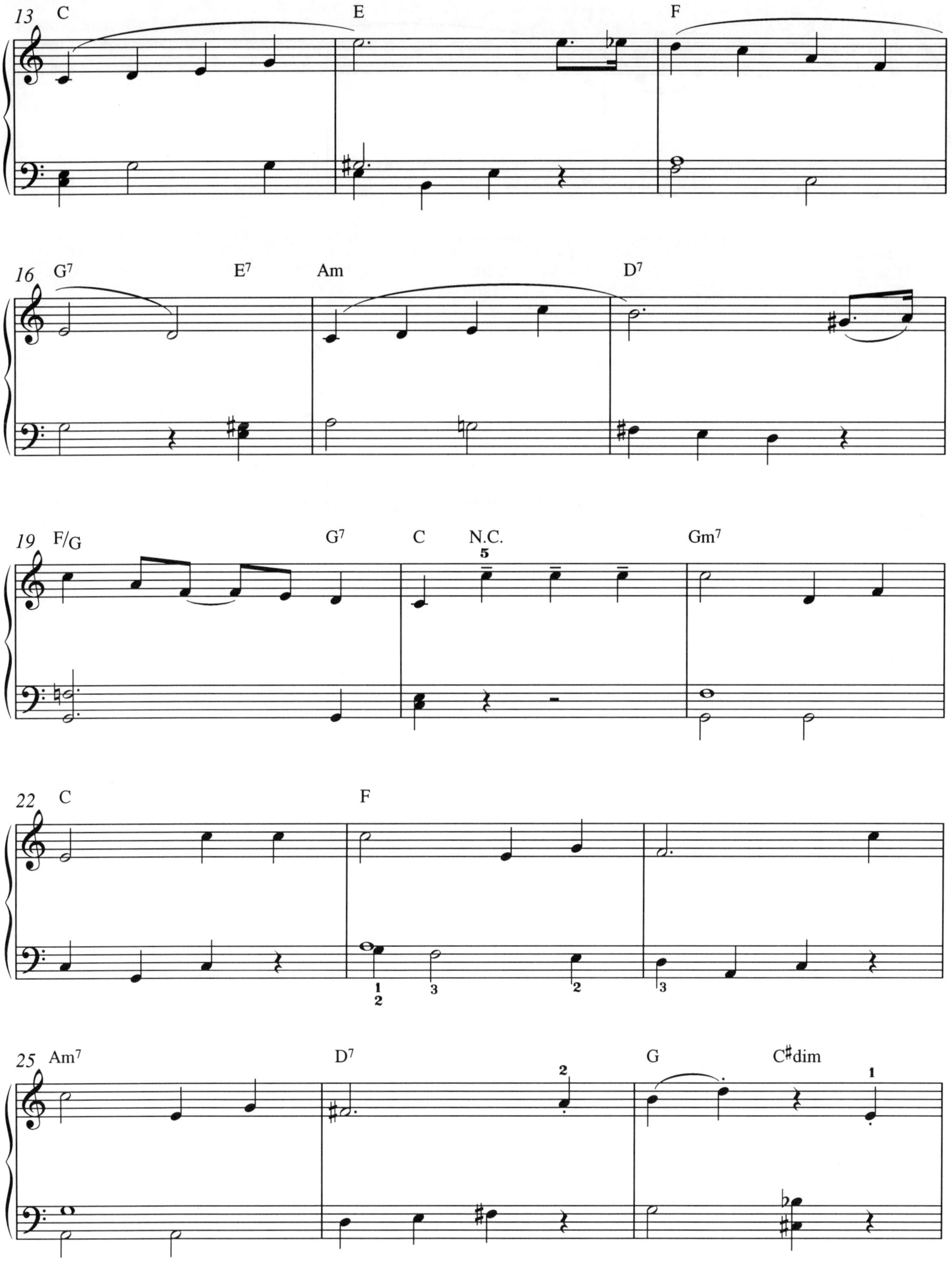
13 C E F
16 G7 E7 Am D7
19 F/G G7 C N.C. Gm7
22 C F
25 Am7 D7 G C♯dim

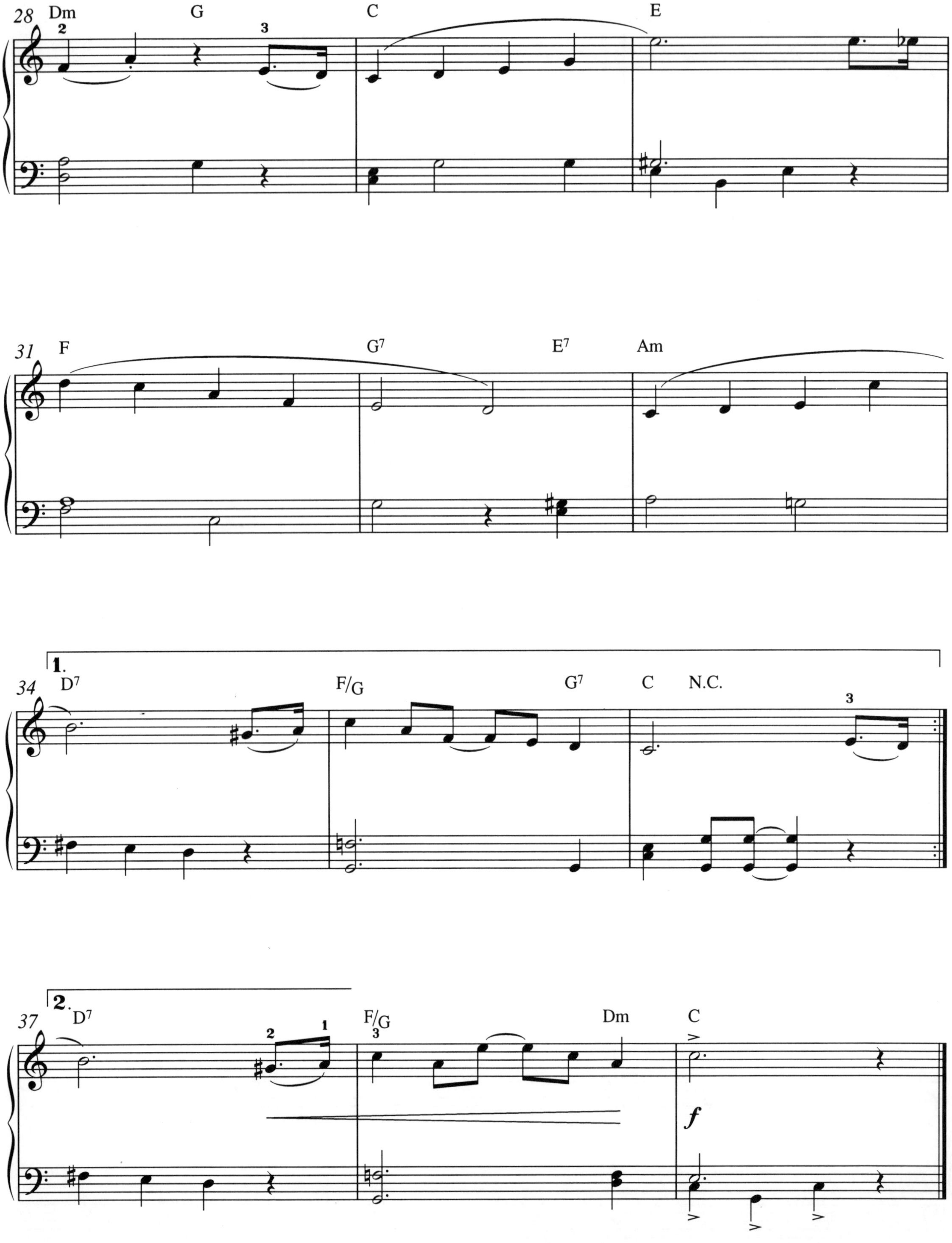
28
Dm
G
C
E
31
F
G7
E7
Am
1.
34
D7
F/G
G7
C
N.C.
2.
37
D7
F/G
Dm
C
f

BETWEEN THE DEVIL AND THE DEEP BLUE SEA

Words by Ted Koehler
Music by Harold Arlen

Notice how, beginning at bar 5, the left hand plays notes on the beat, like a string bass, whilst the right hand plays swing-type phrases. You will need to practice separate hands at first in order to gain fluency in this style of playing.

F6 Gm7 C7aug F
Gm7 C7aug F9 F7(♭9) B♭6 E♭9
Am7 A♭7 Gm7 C7aug F E7 A
Bm7 E9 A6 Cdim Bm7 E13
C Dm7 G9 A♭7 G7 C7
f

29
F6
Gm7
C7aug
F
mf
32
Gm7
C7aug
F9
F7(♭9)
1.
B♭6
E♭9
Am7
A♭7
Gm7 C7aug
3
36
F
Dm7
Gm7
C7aug
2.
B♭6
E♭9
Am7
A♭7
Gm7
N.C.
3
39
E 9/6
F 9/6
ff
1
3
3
1

FRENESI

Music by Alberto Dominguez

There is a touch of Latin about this ballad. It shouldn't be played too fast but at a tempo designed to create a swaying effect.

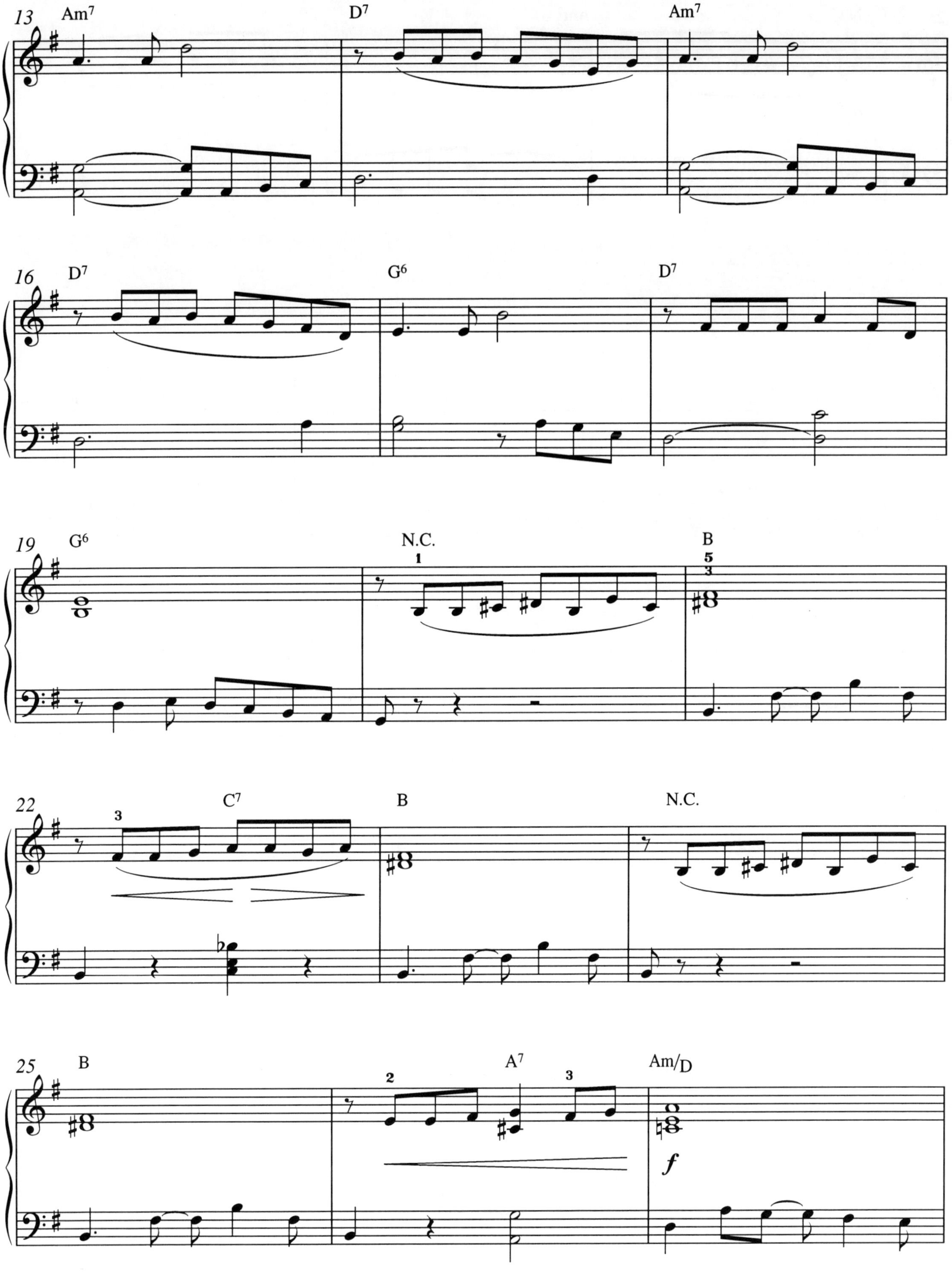
13
Am7
D7
Am7
16
D7
G6
D7
19
G6
N.C.
B
22
C7
B
N.C.
25
B
A7
Am/D
f

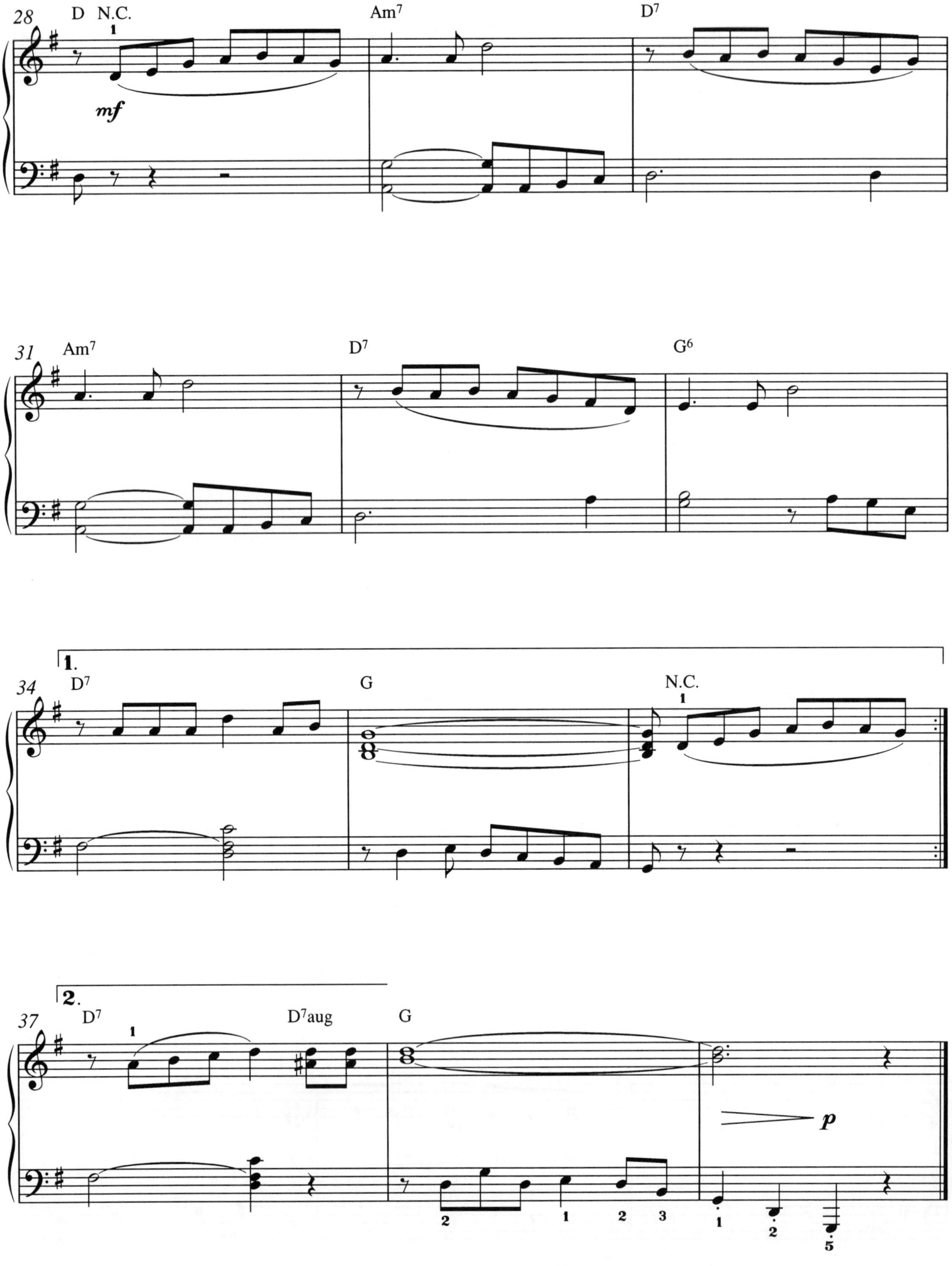
28
D N.C.
mf
Am7
D7
31
Am7
D7
G6
34
1.
D7
G
N.C.
37
2.
D7
D7aug
G
p

HONEYSUCKLE ROSE

Music by Thomas 'Fats' Waller
Words by Andy Razaf

When the tune appears, bar 5 onwards,
try playing the melody notes with a $\frac{12}{8}$ feel.

13
Gm C7 Gm C7 Gm7
16
C7 F G7 C7
19
F Cm7 F9
mp cresc.
22
Bdim F B♭ G♭7 F7 B♭
f
25
Dm7 G9 C♯dim G7 C
p
f

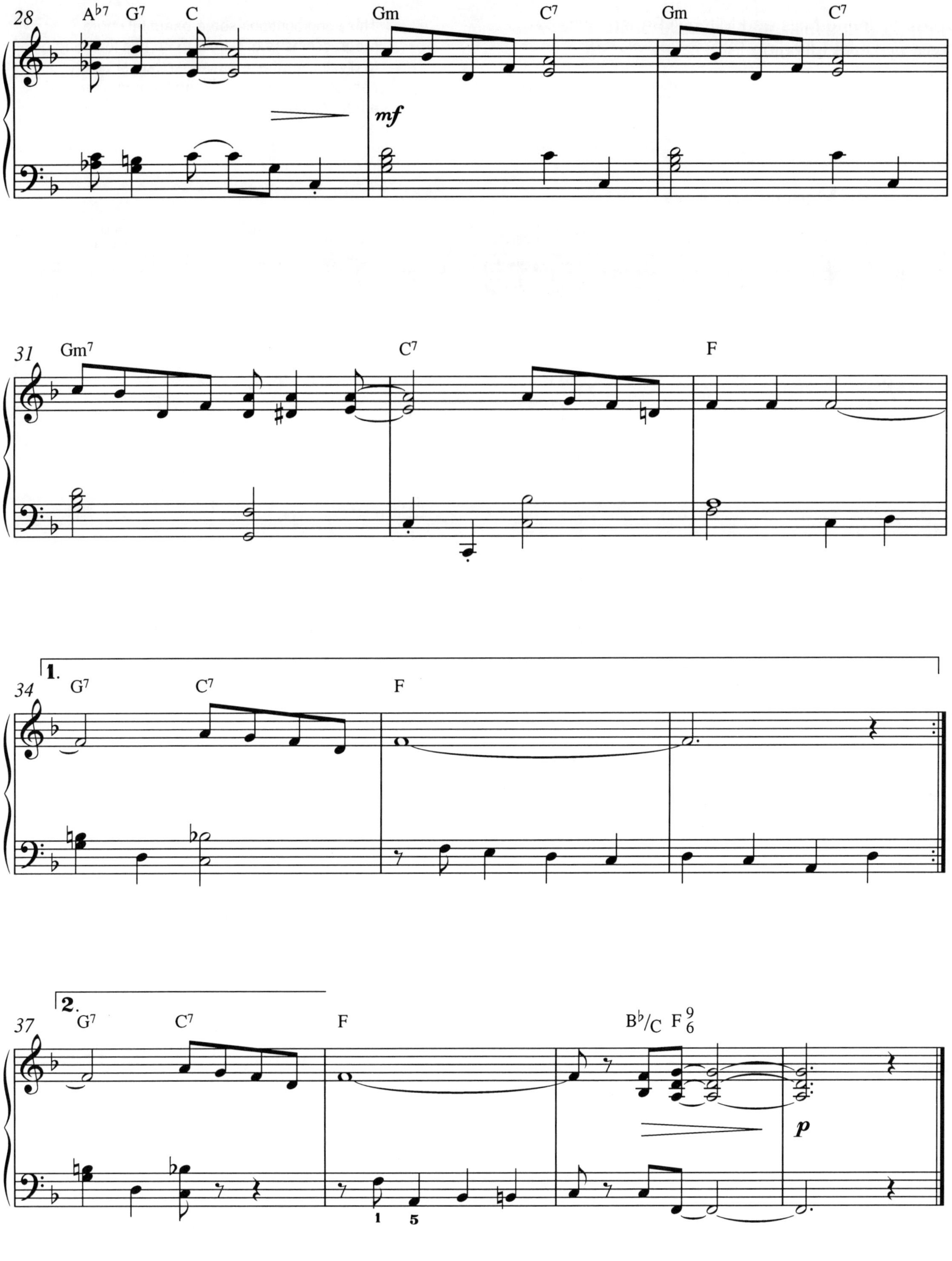
28
A♭7 G7 C
Gm C7
Gm C7
mf
31
Gm7
C7
F
1.
34
G7 C7
F
2.
37
G7 C7
F
B♭/C F 9 6
p
1 5

SOPHISTICATED LADY

Words by Irving Mills and Mitchell Parish
Music by Duke Ellington

This song contains some beautiful chord progressions (e.g. bars 6 to 8). It is tempting to dwell over these passages but, should you choose to do so, try to keep the semblance of a beat going.

13
Fm7
Gm7(♭5)
B7
B♭7
E♭maj7
16
B♭m
C7aug
C7
F7
B♭7
19
E♭maj7
Asus4
A7
D
22
Em7
A7
D
B7
Em7(♭5)
A7(♭9)
25
D
Em7
A7
D
Gm

28
B♭7
G♭m7
Fm7
Gm7(♭5)
B7
B♭7
31
E♭maj7
B♭m
C7aug
C7
F7
1.
34
B♭7
E♭
D♭
C7
2.
37
B♭7
N.C.
D♭9
N.C.
E♭maj9
rit.
p

I'M GETTIN' SENTIMENTAL OVER YOU

Words by Ned Washington
Music by Geo. Bassman

This song provided the band leader Tommy Dorsey with a major hit. Characteristic of the Dorsey sound was a velvety approach when stating the melody. See if you can approximate this effect with your rendition!

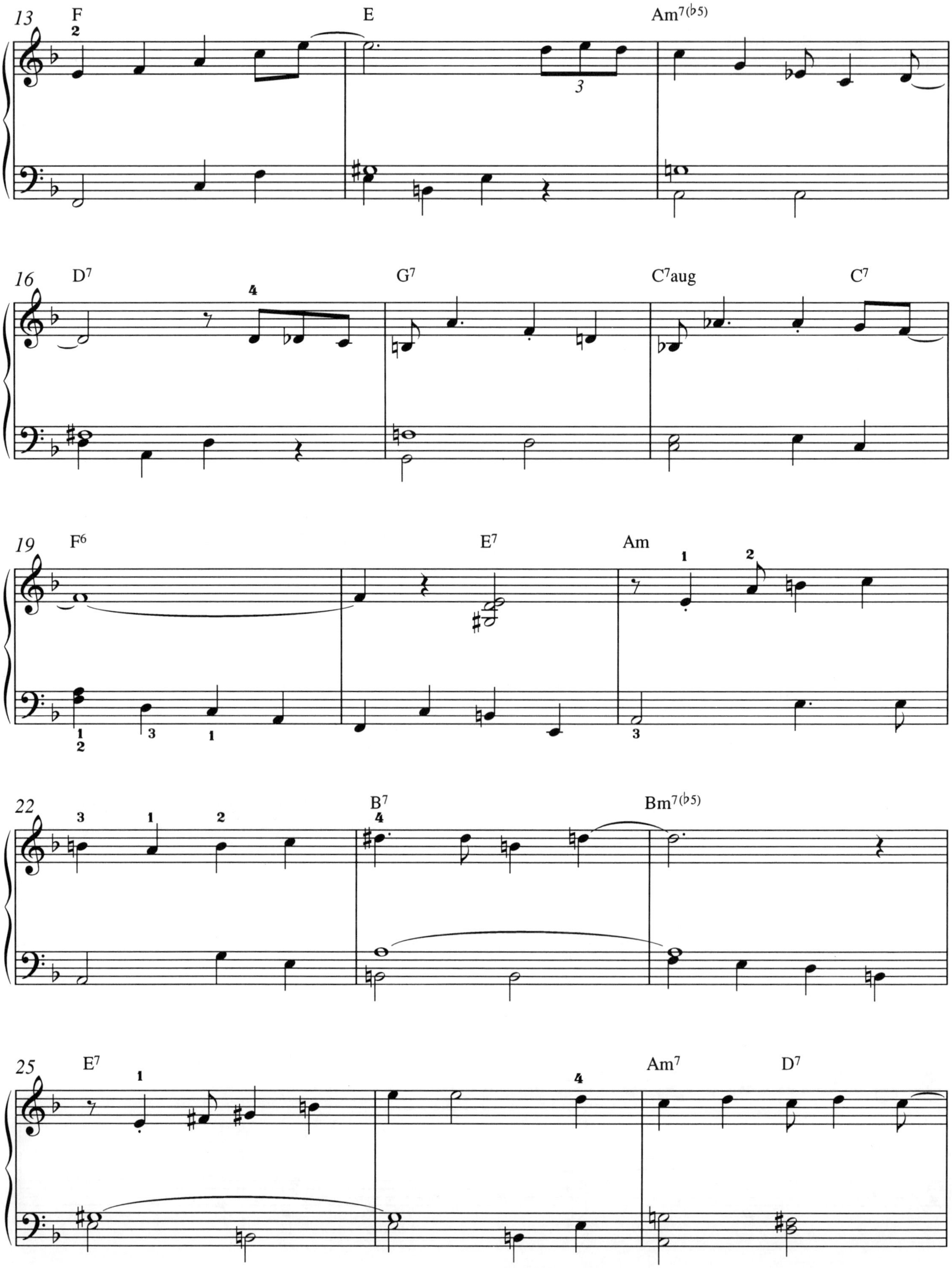
13
F
E
Am7(♭5)
16
D7
G7
C7aug
C7
19
F6
E7
Am
22
B7
Bm7(♭5)
25
E7
Am7
D7

28
Gm7
C7
F
E
3
31
Am7(♭5)
D7
G7
34
C7
C7aug
Fmaj7
D7
1.
37
G7
C7aug
C7
Gm7
A♭dim
F
2.
41
G7
C7
C7aug
C7
B♭6
E♭9
F6
f

I SHOULD CARE

Words and music by Sammy Cahn, Axel Stordahl and
Paul Weston

A gentle treatment suits this fine ballad. Try
putting a slight accent on the third beat of the
melody in bars 5 and 9, etc. Careful use of the
sustaining pedal, i.e. changing pedal when the
harmony changes, will also assist.

16 Bm E7 Em7 A7 Em7 A13
r.h.
20 D6/9 Em7 Em7/A D6/9 F#m7(b5)
24 B7 Em Gm7 C7 Dmaj7
28 C#m7(b5) F#7 Bm(maj7) Bm7 E9 Em9
f
32 A13 G/A A7(b9) 1. D6 B7aug 2. D6
rall.
p

PENNIES FROM HEAVEN

Words by John Burke
Music by Arthur Johnston

This arrangement makes much use of that typical swing/jazz effect: the tied (anticipatory) quaver (the right hand in bar 6 for example). With practice you will learn to play such passages with ease but, initially, practising left and right hands separately will help.

17 D7 G7
21 C Em7 D♯dim Dm7 G7 Dm7 G7
25 C C7 F
30 Fm6 Em7 A7 F
34 D7 G7 1. C6 D7 G7 2. C6 G7 Cmaj9
ff

SATIN DOLL

Words by Johnny Mercer
Music by Duke Ellington and Billy Strayhorn

This song has an in-built feeling of swing about it. Try giving a slight accent to figures beginning on the off-beat, for example the first note of the melody in bar 6 and elsewhere.

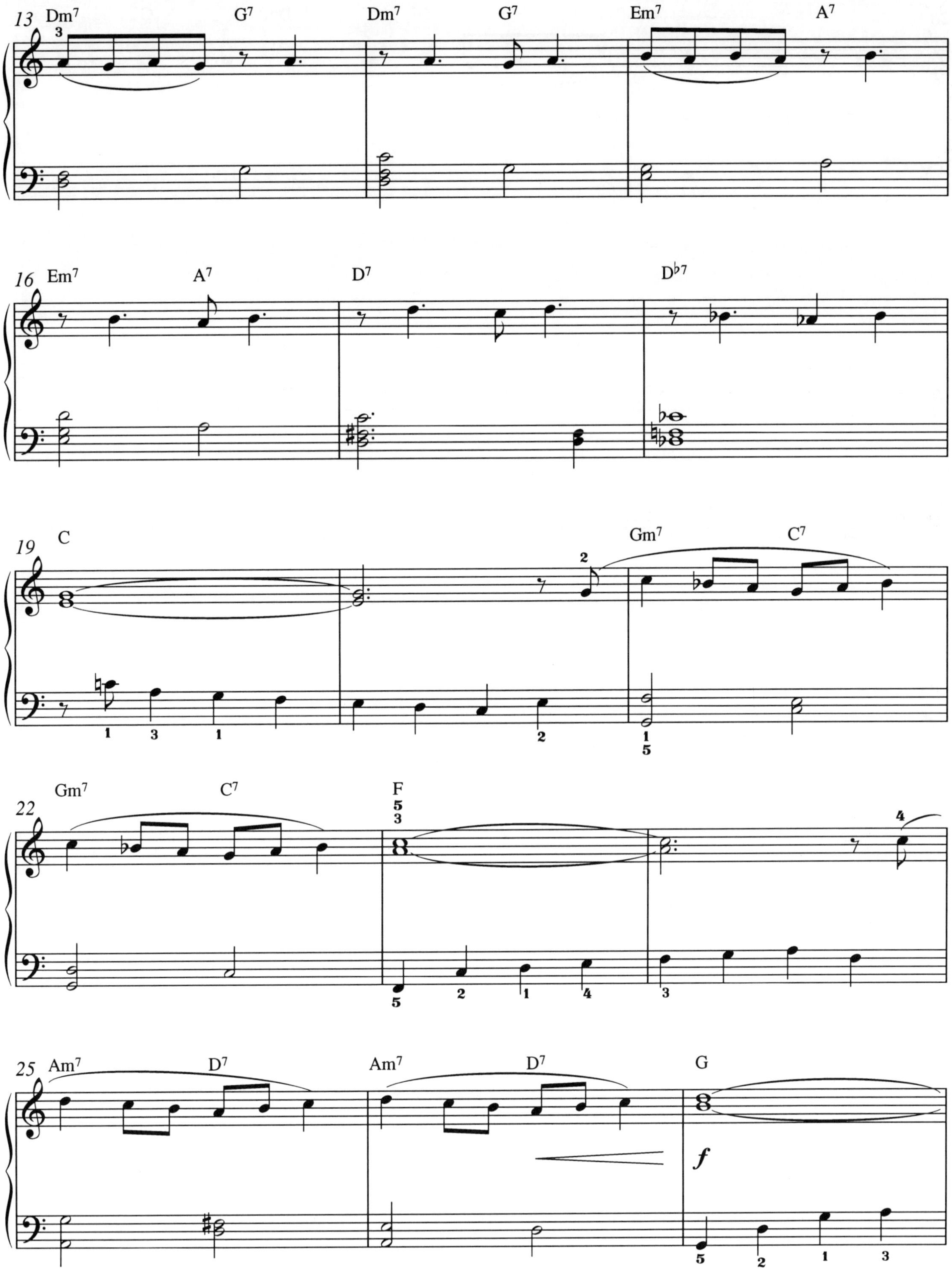
Dm7 G7 Dm7 G7 Em7 A7
Em7 A7 D7 D♭7
C Gm7 C7
Gm7 C7 F
Am7 D7 Am7 D7 G

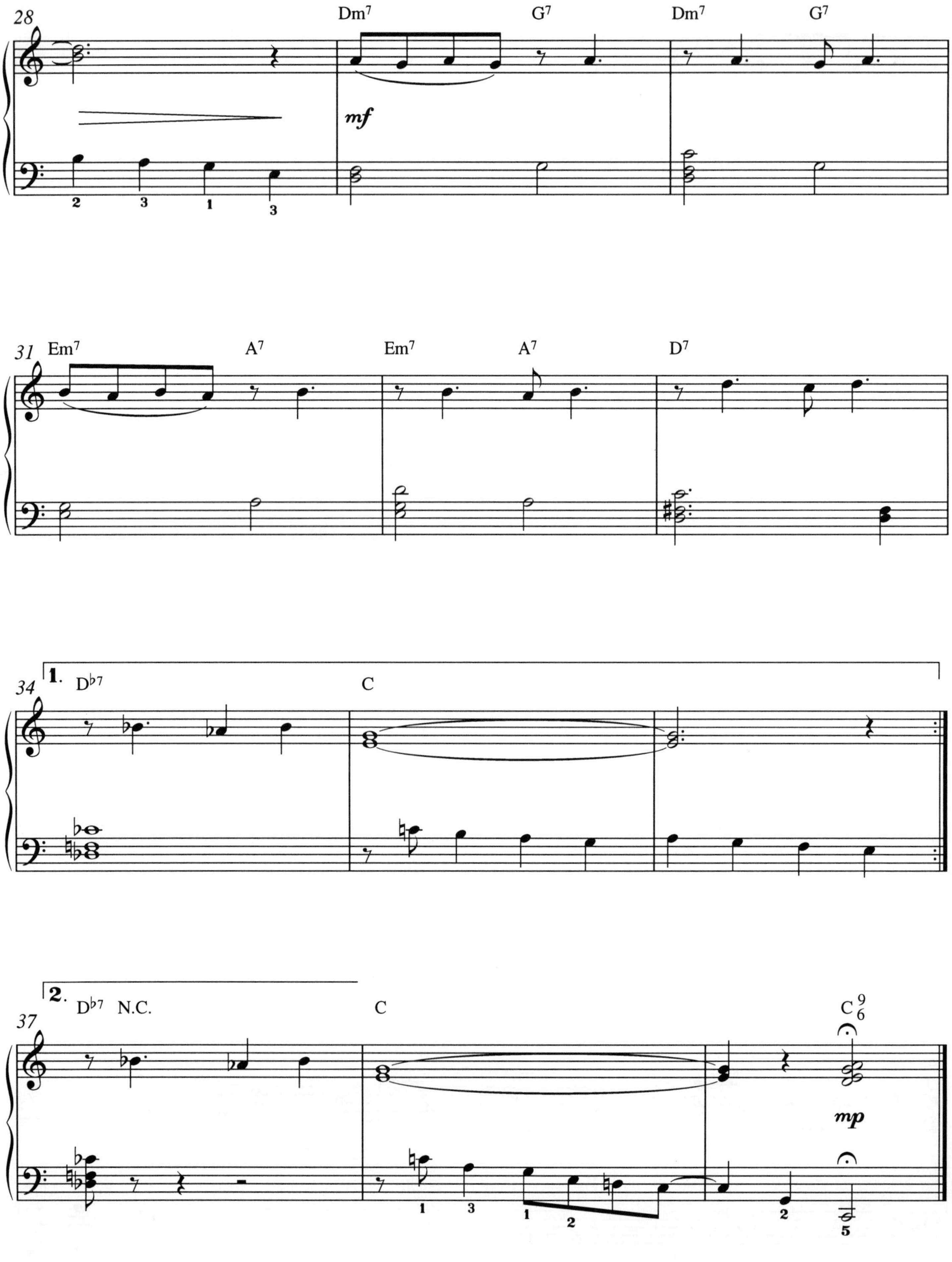
28
Dm7
G7
Dm7
G7
mf
31
Em7
A7
Em7
A7
D7
34
1.
D♭7
C
37
2.
D♭7
N.C.
C
C 6/9
mp

THE NIGHT WE CALLED IT A DAY

Words Tom Adair
Music by Matt Dennis

A warm, tender performance suits this song.
There are passages where the harmonies are
rich, in bars 25 and 39 for example, and all such
passages should sound unhurried.

G
F♯m7
B7(♭9)
Em7
A7
B♭dim
Bm7
B♭9
Am7
D7
G
Am7
D7
Gmaj9
G6
Am7
D9
G6
F♯m7(♭5)
B7
Em7

27
Em7(♭5)
A7
D7sus4
D7
G
F9
30
G
F♯m7
B7(♭9)
Em7
1.
33
Em7
A9
Am7
A♭9
G 9/6
N.C.
f
mp
2.
37
Em7
A9
Am7
B♭/A♭
N.C
G 9/6
f
rall. al fine
pp

PICK YOURSELF UP

Music by Jerome Kern
Words by Dorothy Fields

It is important in this type of piece to maintain a crisp sense of rhythm. Left hand figures, for example the last two notes in bar 6, should be played lightly.

13
Dm7 G7 Cmaj7 Fmaj7 Bm7(♭5) E7(♭9)
16
Am7 D9 Dm7 G7 Dm7 G7
19
Dm7 G7 C To Coda D♭
f
22
25
F

28
B9(♭5)
Cm7
F7
B♭maj7
E♭maj7
mf
31
Am7(♭5)
D7(♭9)
Gm7
C7
Cm7
F7
34
Cm7
F7
Cm7
F7
B♭
D.S. al Coda
CODA
37
D♭
f
40
F

43
B9(♭5)
Cm7
F7
mf
46
B♭maj7
E♭maj7
Am7(♭5)
D7(♭9)
Gm7
C7
Cm7
F7
50
Cm7
F7
Cm7
F7
Fm6/G
G7(♯5)
53
Cm7
F9
B♭6
B9(♭5)
B♭13(♯11)
B♭13
ff

NIGHT TRAIN

Words by Oscar Washington and Lewis C. Simpkins
Music by Jimmy Forrest

This piece benefits from being played in an extrovert, flag-waving style. Nevertheless, to sound really effective, make sure you maintain the underlying rhythm strictly throughout.

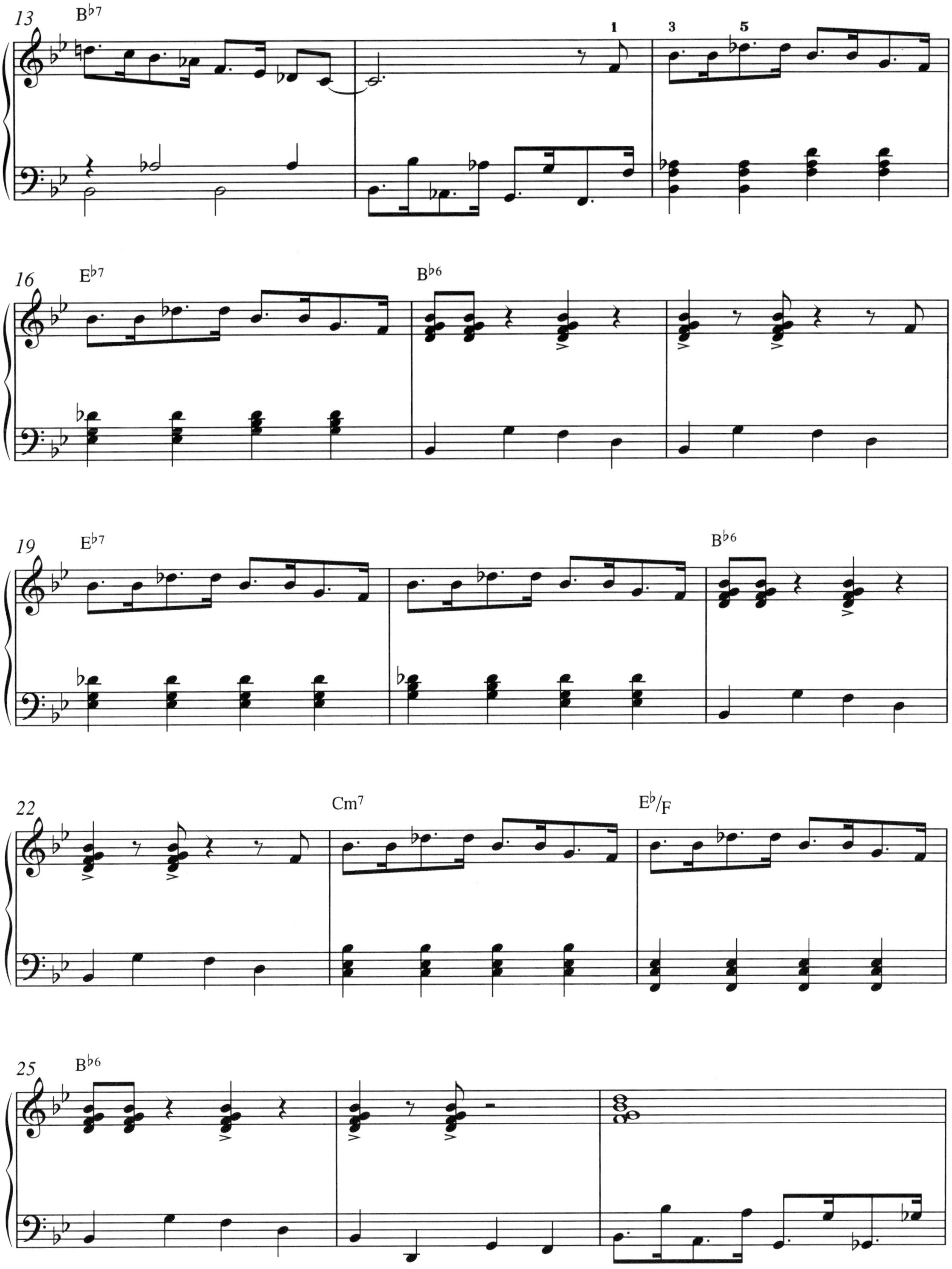
13
B♭7
1 3 5
16
E♭7
B♭6
19
E♭7
B♭6
22
Cm7
E♭/F
25
B♭6

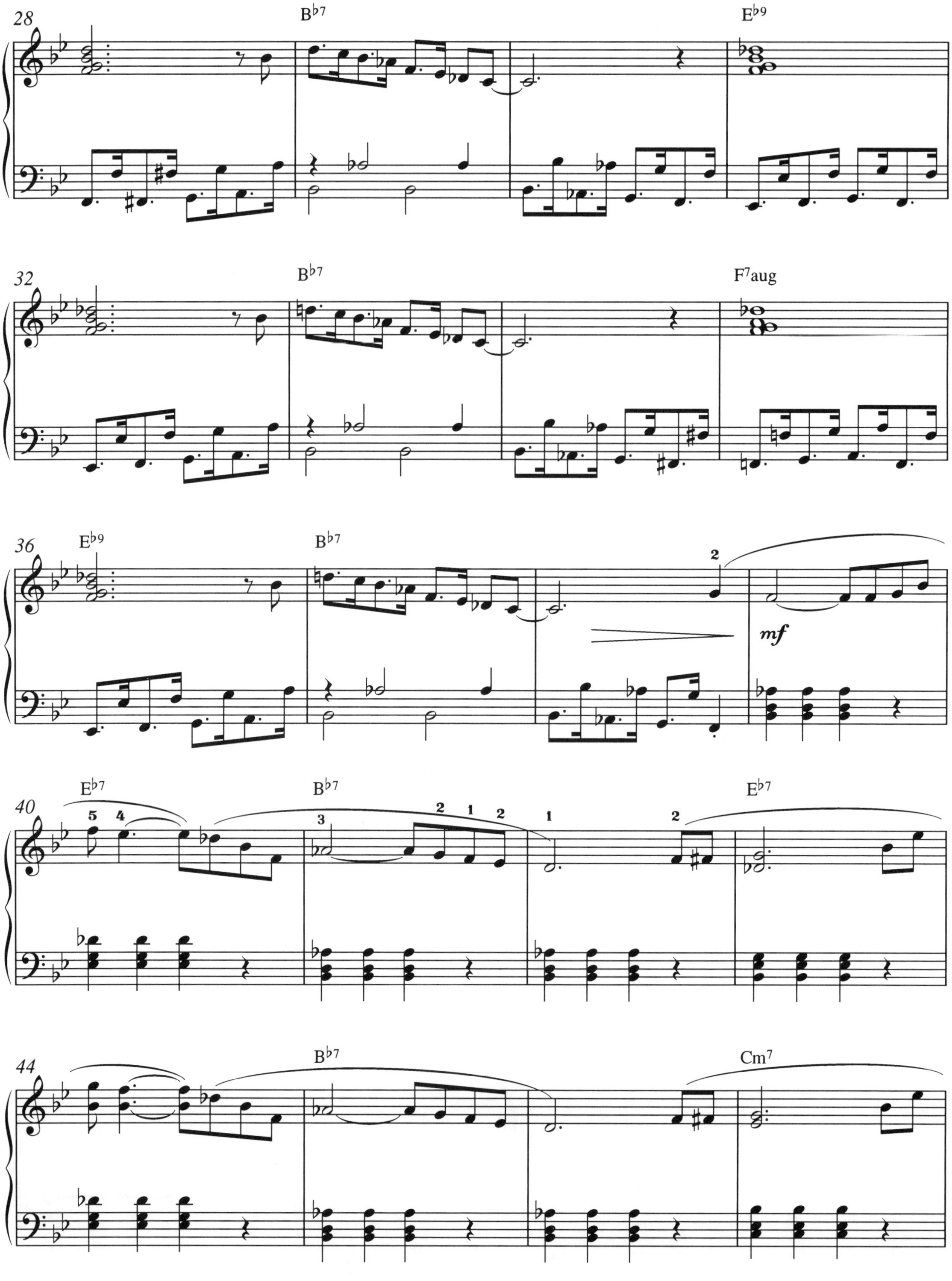
28
B♭7
E♭9
32
B♭7
F7aug
36
E♭9
B♭7
mf
40
E♭7
B♭7
E♭7
44
B♭7
Cm7

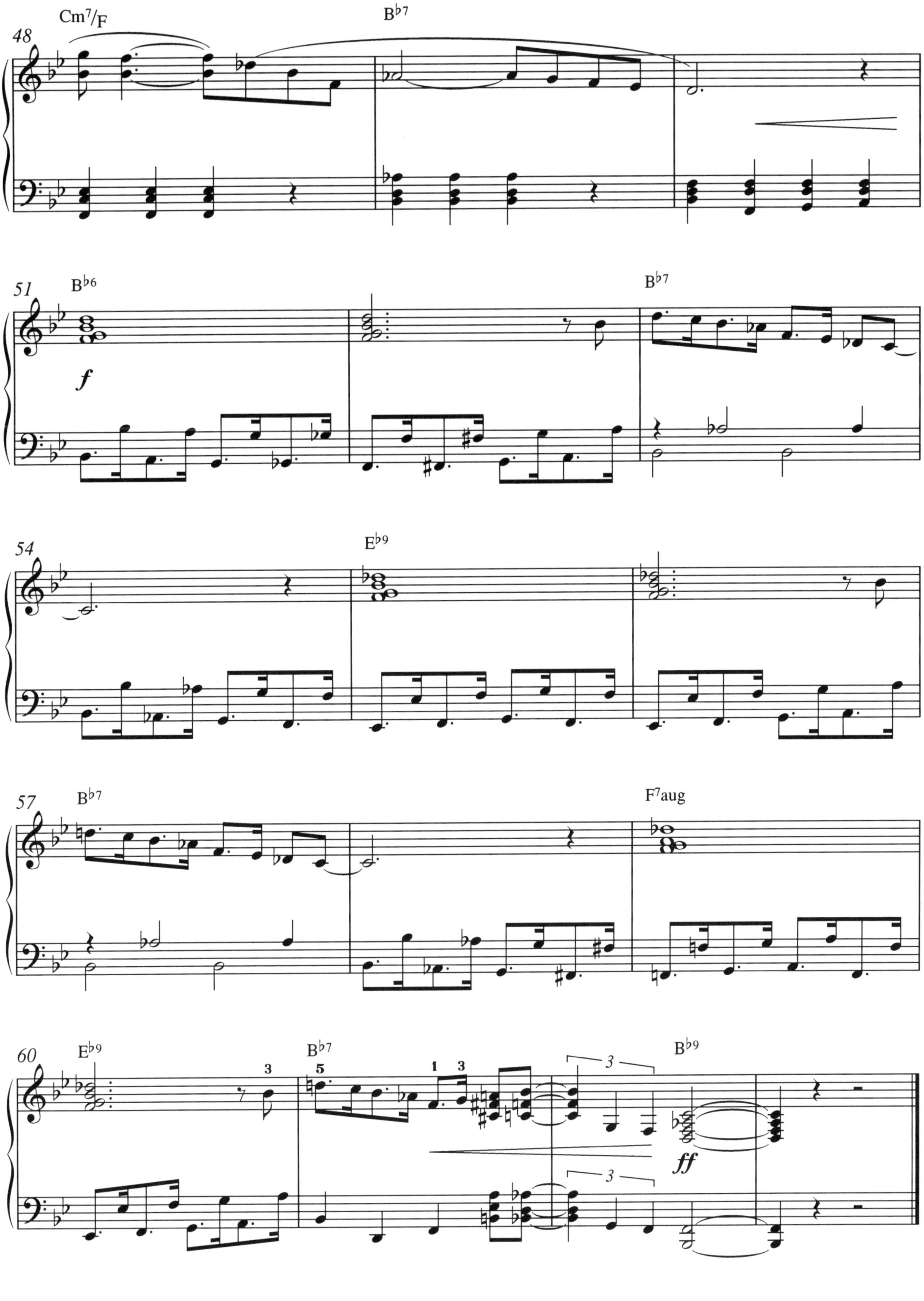
48
Cm7/F
B♭7
51
B♭6
f
B♭7
54
E♭9
57
B♭7
F7aug
60
E♭9
B♭7
3
B♭9
ff

COME FLY WITH ME

Words by Sammy Cahn
Music by Jimmy Van Heusen

This arrangement has echoes of big band swing.
Try putting accents on the second and fourth
beats, e.g. in bars 13 and 14, to suggest a
drummer stressing the off-beats.

19
Dm7
G7
C
C7
23
F
B♭9
C
F7
27
C
N.C.
A♭
A♭aug
A♭6
D♭maj 9 6
D♭
32
E♭9
A♭
N.C.
37
A♭
A♭aug
A♭6
G

41 Am7 D7 G7 F♯7 F7 E7 E♭7 D7 D♭7 N.C.
mp mf
45 C Em7 E♭dim Dm7 G7
49 C C7 F B♭9
53 C F7 Cmaj7 B♭7 A7 D9
58 F/G Ddim C6 C6 C 9 6
1. 2.
ff mf fff